My First RODEO

BARREL RACING

Rochelle Groskreutz

AV2
www.av2books.com

Step 1
Go to **www.av2books.com**

Step 2
Enter this unique code
HUDOS5T46

Step 3
Explore your interactive eBook!

AV2 is optimized for use on any device

Your interactive eBook comes with...

- Read — **Audio** Listen to the entire book read aloud
- **Videos** Watch informative video clips
- **Weblinks** Gain additional information for research
- **Try This!** Complete activities and hands-on experiments
- **Key Words** Study vocabulary, and complete a matching word activity
- **Quizzes** Test your knowledge
- **Slideshows** View images and captions

View new titles and product videos at www.av2books.com

BARREL RACING

Contents

I am at my first rodeo.
I want to see the
barrel racing event.

Barrel racing is the **only rodeo event** to be created for **women.**

BARREL RACING
10.1
10.1

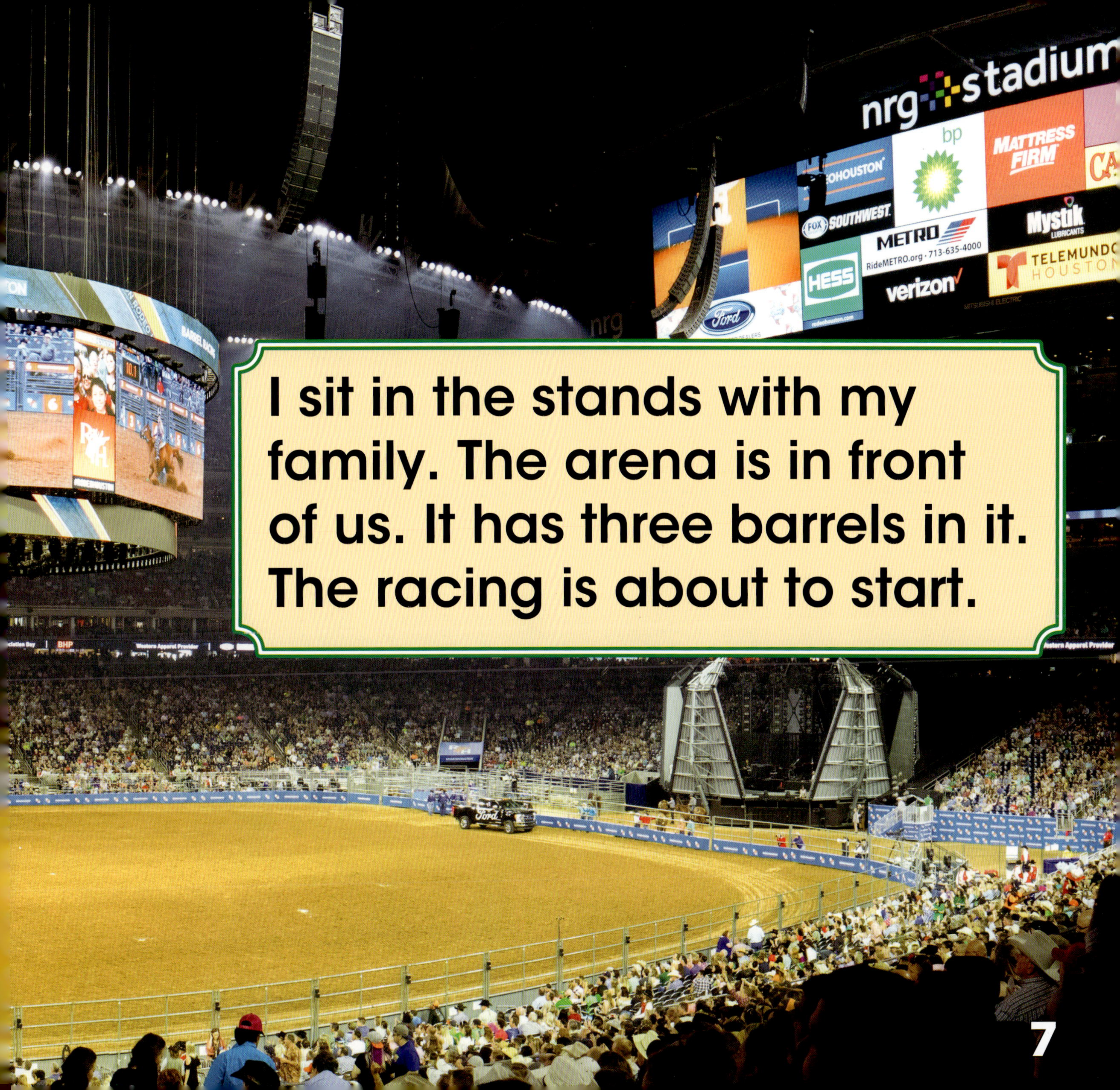

I sit in the stands with my family. The arena is in front of us. It has three barrels in it. The racing is about to start.

The first rider is on her horse. They look ready to race.

The reins are used to steer the horse and tell it what to do.

The bridle links the reins to the horse.

The saddle helps the rider stay on her horse.

Boots protect the horse's hooves and legs.

The rider urges her horse to a gallop. They run past the starting line. The race is on.

A **barrel racing** team should be at **top speed** before they **cross** the starting line.

OOT BARN
Live West
bootbarn.com

The team races toward the first barrel. The rider steers the horse in a tight circle around one side of the barrel.

They charge toward the second barrel. The horse circles this barrel from the other side.

LAKOTA
BONANZA
COME
FANS

HEATING
(530) 365-
ANDERSON, CA

The rider rushes her horse toward the third barrel. She knows that they must be careful.

They can not have any of the barrels tip over.

A team has **5 seconds** added to its time for **every tipped** barrel.

The barrel stays up!

The rider runs her horse back to the starting line as fast as she can.

The rider looks to the clock for her time.

She knows she will win the event if no one goes around the barrels faster than her.

July 15, 2018
Ladies Barrel Racing Champion
$100,000.00
PAY TO THE ORDER OF HAILEY KINSEL
One Hundred Thousand /100 DOLLARS

BARREL RACING

FUN FACTS

The **first official** barrel racing contest was held in **1948** in **Texas.**

The **world champions** of barrel racing have ranged in **age** from **10 to 58**.

A **barrel racing team** can reach **speeds** of more than **30 miles** (48 kilometers) per hour.

Top barrel racers can **earn more than $300,000** per year.

Barrels must be **55 gallons** (208 liters) in size.

Barrel racers make a **3-leaf clover pattern** when they circle **the barrels**.

KEY WORDS

Research has shown that as much as 65 percent of all written material published in English is made up of 300 words. These 300 words cannot be taught using pictures or learned by sounding them out. They must be recognized by sight. This book contains 72 common sight words to help young readers improve their reading fluency and comprehension. This book also teaches young readers several important content words, such as proper nouns. These words are paired with pictures to aid in learning and improve understanding.

Page	Sight Words First Appearance
4	am, at, first, I, my, see, the, to, want
5	be, for, is, only
7	about, family, has, in, it, of, start, three, us, with
8	and, are, do, her, look, on, tell, they, used, what
9	helps
10	a, before, line, run, should
13	around, one, side
14	from, other, second, this
17	any, can, every, have, its, knows, must, not, over, she, that, time
19	as, back, up
20	if, no, than, will
22	was, world
23	make, miles, more, when, year

Page	Content Words First Appearance
4	barrel racing event, rodeo
5	women
7	arena, barrels, stands
8	horse, reins, rider
9	boots, bridle, hooves, legs, saddle
10	gallop, speed, team
13	circle
20	clock
22	age, champions, contest, Texas
23	gallons, hour, pattern, size

Published by AV2
276 5th Avenue, Suite 704 #917
New York, NY 10001
Website: www.av2books.com

Library of Congress Cataloging-in-Publication Data
Names: Groskreutz, Rochelle, author. | AV2 by Weigl.
Title: Barrel racing / Rochelle Groskreutz and Heather Kissock.
Description: New York : AV^2, 2020. | Series: My First Rodeo | Audience: Ages 5-8 years | Audience: Grades K-1
Identifiers: LCCN 2020004069 (print) | LCCN 2020004070 (ebook) | ISBN 9781791123963 (Library Binding) | ISBN 9781791123970 (Paperback) | ISBN 9781791123987 (eBook) | ISBN 9781791123994
Subjects: LCSH: Barrel racing--Juvenile literature. | Rodeos--Juvenile literature.
Classification: LCC GV1834.45.B35 G76 2020 (print) | LCC GV1834.45.B35 (ebook) | DDC 791.8/4--dc23
LC record available at https://lccn.loc.gov/2020004069
LC ebook record available at https://lccn.loc.gov/2020004070

Printed in Guangzhou, China
2 3 4 5 6 7 8 9 0 27 26 25 24 23

062023
230602

Project Coordinator: Heather Kissock Designer: Ana María Vidal

AV2 acknowledges Getty, iStock, Shutterstock, and Alamy as the primary image suppliers for this title.